You'll Get There
Samantha Elizabeth Parrell

Illustration

You'll Get There Copyright © 2021 Samantha Elizabeth Parrell
All rights reserved. No part of this book may be used, sold or copied without the author's explicit consent except for the use of quotes and excerpts for the purpose of reviews and articles.

Illustrations by Megan Nicole McNeil

ISBN: 978-1-7779378-2-9

Anchored to an island,
spending most days by the ocean.

These pages are filled with waves of my emotions,
connected to this place.

Authors Note

I simply do not run out of things to say,
the words are just bottled up
and thrown to sea.
Instead of sharing them with others,
out of fear of drowning in judgment.

Table of Contents

Land - Body 01

Headland - Heart 23

Waves - Thoughts 47

Corrasion - Tiny Victories 69

Abrasion - Larger Impacts 91

Land - Body

Samantha Elizabeth Parrell

The land started bare
it grew into itself over time
using all of its features to stay alive.

Similar to myself.

You'll Get There

The process to get there
simply put
has been one collision after the next.

Only I can create
from what is on my plate
by pushing upward
and forming under the pressure.

Samantha Elizabeth Parrell

I've never been content
with the way the land shapes under my feet.

I've explored
ways to carve the ridges
to find my true self.

You'll Get There

I've inherited
the ability to feel
when the rain is coming.

My body aches
when the weather changes.

The landscape
is easier to navigate
when it's familiar.

People often revisit places
when they feel like home.

You'll Get There

When the infatuation of exploring
wears away
you'll see that
this difficult land
has wrinkles and scars.

Will you stay?

Samantha Elizabeth Parrell

Nobody notices the sun
when it's behind the clouds.

I notice your effort
to make my day a little brighter
when my body doesn't feel like mine.

You'll Get There

When seeds are planted correctly
growth
comes with time.

They always said
they bloomed with pride
when they spoke of me.

But, I know that I still have much growth to do.

Samantha Elizabeth Parrell

Nine chances out of ten
when the compass is pointed in the opposite direction
my body vibrates
my resentment rises.

My mind gets lost
in the fog
in the forest ahead.

You'll Get There

When exploring
those darker parts of the forest.

Sometimes
it would take days
to find my way back out.

You could tell
from the exhaustion on my face
that I got lost
in who I thought I was supposed to be along the way.

Samantha Elizabeth Parrell

"Let's go on an adventure."

It's almost as if you knew
I'd struggle with your demons
before you were ready to face them.

My ability to absorb your every emotion
has forced me
to bury mine in the dirt.

When speaking with others
I shy away from showing them
the x on the ground.

Maybe one day
I'll dig those feelings up.

You'll Get There

Your hand
that hike
my fear of heights
conquered.

Because you knew
even before I could realize
that my mind
would overcome my weakness
and it did.

Samantha Elizabeth Parrell

My mind
it climbs those stairs
before my emotions are able to catch up.

Perhaps that's why
my heart
feels like it's ready to burst
when individuals
show me acceptance.

For others
my lungs can taste
the salt they leave behind
with their judgement.

You'll Get There

The map
of another person's journey
is easiest to view.

You can admire their route
from afar.

No judgement
just astonishment
of how far they have made it
without getting lost.

Samantha Elizabeth Parrell

Have you ever explored a cellar?

Thoughts of how you look
to others
can be stored there
during the winter.

The sun
it helps to process
what you will find
when you're ready to open the door
in warmer temperatures.

I always preferred the colder months.

You'll Get There

I've been told
not to respond
in the moment.

It's easiest
to clear my vision
and respond with my heart
in time.

Samantha Elizabeth Parrell

The endurance of my thoughts
can cloud my body's ability to move.

On days like today
I force myself to visit the ocean
to find clarity in the chaos.

You'll Get There

I have to sit
in a field of thought
before my heart
moves on
and my feet
start to wander
again.

Samantha Elizabeth Parrell

The resistance of human skin
depends on its habits.

Mine is delicate
it wouldn't be prepared
for the electricity flowing through it.

This shock
wouldn't even make it
through your skin.
You'd stay unharmed
you'd move on to the next thrill.

You'll Get There

I can sense it coming
I am attracted to it
and wait for it to be produced again.

I always loved the smell of rain.

Geosmin
has a funny way of
bringing a sense of calm
related to the trails I travel on
to clear my thoughts.

Headland - Heart

Samantha Elizabeth Parrell

That feeling.

It's the warmth
rushing through my veins.

The weight
of the water lifted from my chest.

The wind
brushing past my cheeks.

The mere sound
of relief
as the ocean pulls back
just for a moment
from the coast.

You'll Get There

Anchored between two boats.

One ready to set sail
the other anchored to the shore.

I've never been named
after a build.

I prefer it that way.

Samantha Elizabeth Parrell

Over the years
my heart has crashed
over and over.

Yet some form of light
whether from a sunrise or sunset
has kept it from sinking entirely.

You'll Get There

I always enjoyed thunder and lightning storms.

It's likely the reason why
I don't shy away from a shipwreck.

Samantha Elizabeth Parrell

You knew that one day
I would look to travel alone
on the current that the waves created.

You knew that my path would be turbulent.
It would get even more complicated with time.

You saw the warning signs.

I think that's why you learned to fly a plane.
So that you could see my path clearly
and wait to meet me at the end.

You'll Get There

"You're not a burden."

On the days when
the heaviness of my thoughts
created an undertow
and I felt like I was drowning in the ocean.

I needed to learn
to lean into those four words
to let you hold that weight
just for a moment.

Samantha Elizabeth Parrell

I could feel your eyes
creating tidal waves
of thought around commitment.

But my ability to knock you off
that steady surface
sometimes made you frustrated
with continuing to surf.

You'll Get There

"It's okay to need someone."

An independent woman
with a soul that loves to adventure on her own.

I had to let those words
sink in.

Samantha Elizabeth Parrell

You signed up to spend
the best years of your life
at sea.

I signed up to spend mine
thanking you
for showing me
that young love
can turn into a friendship.

You'll Get There

You were clean drinking water
a little too defined for my taste.

Samantha Elizabeth Parrell

The reality
of how cold the water was
when you swam in your feelings
alone
shocked you.

I kept my distance
from the cold waters.

I'd rather feel the warmth.

I guess the others
were willing to drown in the ocean
for you.

I think you preferred it that way.

You'll Get There

My arms were tired
from always climbing the mountain
to find you first.

So, I sat on a rock
watched the waves crash along the coastline
and waited.

This gave me time to separate
my head from my heart.

I'm glad I built that strength
because you finally hiked to me.

Samantha Elizabeth Parrell

It takes time
to find the bottom of the ocean floor.

I warned you
as I sank.

It's the beauty
of the detachment style.

You'll Get There

When my heart
doesn't need you anymore.
It'll get quiet.

The kind of peace you find
right before a hurricane.

You'll miss the loud.

When the waves crash
and flood the streets.

I'll be nowhere to be found.

Samantha Elizabeth Parrell

You only wanted me
as an ocean surface level
of a distraction.

I wanted the diversity
of the conversation.

But you were sensitive
to climate change.

You'll Get There

Maybe love
is just a side effect.

Sparked by
the accidental gulp of minerals
found in the plunge
of going into the deep sea.

I'd prefer the pungent reek of the surface layer.

Samantha Elizabeth Parrell

There are so many expectations.

It's a wonder
that there are couples
who brave the onslaught.

I'd rather live
in the microbial ocean
where the diversity of my emotions
can stay unknown.

You'll Get There

Midnight marathon conversations
with intelligent, creative people.

The intense appreciation
of honesty.

I believe passion
is the most beautiful trait
a person can possess.

Samantha Elizabeth Parrell

I avoided swimming
away from the shoreline.

My landmark
was always your heart.

If I couldn't see that.
If it was impossible to reach
I would have put myself in danger
of drowning.

You'll Get There

An over-thinker
prepares
their anxious mind
for the lakes and rivers
beneath the ocean's surface.

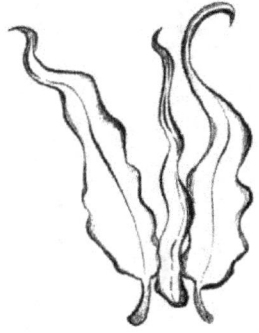

Samantha Elizabeth Parrell

I just want to be a coral.

But, we know what happens to coral
when it's under attack.

You'll Get There

You held on to the sand
I left in your hands.

It took ten years
for you to form
a sandcastle
shaped as an apology.

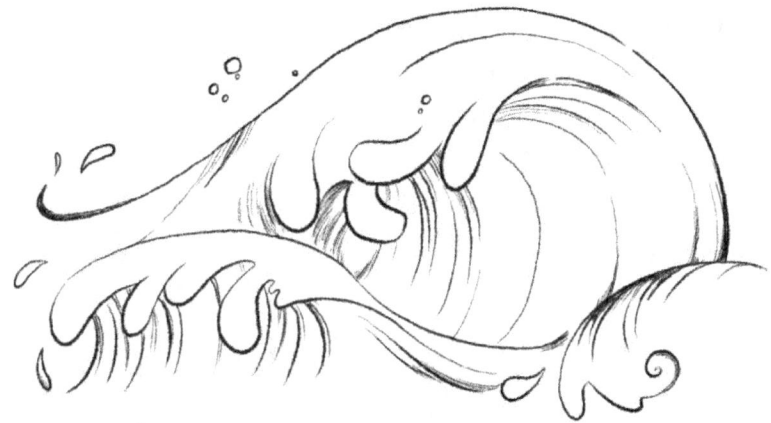

Waves - Thoughts

Don't forget
oil floats above water.

When you're putting out fires
other's have started with a match
sink into the depths of the ocean
let the salt water soak in.

Don't let them burn you.

You'll Get There

I put on my bravest face
when I'm in my darkest moments.

A smile
will leave them believing
in sunsets
and moments
of golden bliss.

It will hide
the rough waves that occured
in the early hours.

Samantha Elizabeth Parrell

Asking questions
can be intrusive.

Perhaps it is because
valleys were created by storms.

And if someone explored my caves
they will find a lot
of unanswered questions hidden.

You'll Get There

One shift
in the current
of your thoughts
and my entire approach
to our conversation
will change.

Samantha Elizabeth Parrell

My mind was jolted
with the temperature of the ocean water
as I tried to jump right in.

After a year
I was only ready to dip my toe in.

Now
I feel like I'm drowning once again.

You've pulled me into
the depths of what was.

My emotions
are trying to align
with my mind's reaction
to the safety I created.

You'll Get There

I don't do well under pressure.

Expectations
I fall short of them.

Or at least I think I do
because I don't see what you see.
I only see me.

Samantha Elizabeth Parrell

The hardest
and most painful part
of this realization
was to swallow the knowledge
that I will never be able to please everyone.

You'll Get There

Daughter of the king of mermaids, mindset.

Like the sea,
I can be a little salty.

Samantha Elizabeth Parrell

When a wave breaks a rock
over and over again
there's a moment
to save the rock from abrasion.

Sometimes
it's not saying everything you want to say
but making room for others to think.

You'll Get There

You spoke softly
and with confidence.

You pointed out
that I always over packed.

But, I wanted to be prepared
for the moment you didn't show interest
in the planning stages of our trip.

I will always over pack.

Samantha Elizabeth Parrell

You are there for them
when they need your advice
yet some do not reciprocate.

Do not let this change
how you treat others
or yourself.

You'll Get There

My grandmother left some
knowledge
tradition
and wisdom
behind in my blood.

Samantha Elizabeth Parrell

Not based on looks or ability
but the condition of the heart.

The comfort of being alone.

You'll Get There

I am now awash with feelings
sentiments
sensations
and most interestingly
a longing.

Samantha Elizabeth Parrell

The red ruby slipper
with no home to return to.

You'll Get There

Put your life on pause.
Pause it.
Look at the still scene in front of you.
What do you see?

I am a background actress in a film
on a screen in a small hometown theatre.

I've never been one to make the scene.

Imagine
there was nothing holding you back.

Imagine
that poor circumstances weren't there.

Imagine
the impossibility of failure.

You'll Get There

Even amidst
all of the noise
your voice
calmed my chaotic thoughts.

Samantha Elizabeth Parrell

It's a truth
beyond the reality
we are so comfortable in.

Where mistakes
are easily forgiven
and we can always try again.

You'll Get There

And while you're still here.

Love acts
Fear reacts.

Unfortunately for most
fear has become the dictator.

Corrasion - Tiny Victories

Samantha Elizabeth Parrell

I'm strong enough
to withstand my inner storm.
I'd label that
an accomplishment.

You'll Get There

You left our childhood on a sweet note
a friendship never forgotten
and a laughter that echoes
in the caves of our memories.

Samantha Elizabeth Parrell

Navigating
finding you
in what I do.

You'll Get There

And in my boldest moments
as if I were diving off of a cliff
to swim against my fears
I think and see clearly.

Samantha Elizabeth Parrell

It struck me like lighting
that there is an overzealous emphasis
on creating a grandiose display
that celebrates the start of something.

You'll Get There

My family
an amazing source of encouragement.

They take the pebbles of their experience
to shelter me from the largest waves.

I let the seaweed of their knowledge
shape my decisions.

Though jellyfish
have stung me a few times
along the way.

Samantha Elizabeth Parrell

Vulnerability.
That's the landslide.

The scraping
and scratching
and scouring.

I've cleared away the experiences
the moments that have shaped me into who I am today.

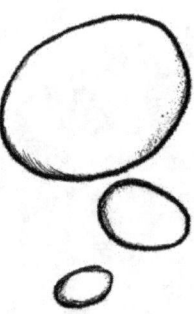

You'll Get There

I think relationships are all about compromise
finding an equilibrium
that allows both people to feel comfortable
and happy.

Samantha Elizabeth Parrell

Not thinking
not feeling
just calm and sedate.

You'll Get There

With only the sound
of our own slowing hearts
beating in our ears.

Samantha Elizabeth Parrell

That Landwash.

It's like the mound of clothes on the floor
unwashed hair
the darkest moments
throughout the busiest seasons.

Getting out of bed on these days
I make my way to the oceans edge
to breathe in that fresh air
to find the light.

You'll Get There

Hurling experience
over education
at anyone willing to take a chance
on a woman
with a lot of determination
and willing to help others.

Samantha Elizabeth Parrell

Consciously prepared
for those who throw pebbles.

But more aware of those
who sorts pebbles into piles.

You'll Get There

The pause
A millisecond.

You still caught that slight sudden stop.

The kind of stop even heard at sea.

Samantha Elizabeth Parrell

And to really know me
is to not only look at the outside
but the inside too.

There's a different kind of beauty in vulnerability
than in strength.

You'll Get There

There's a lot we can learn from trees
mostly
their ability to withstand years of materials hurled at them.

Waiting to be appreciated
by a wiser eye.

Samantha Elizabeth Parrell

Understanding inequalities
continuously listening.

I am always willing to learn.

You'll Get There

Shared sense of injustice.
Well-meaning.
Imperfect.

Movement of unity.
Guilt.
Shame.

You'll Get There

Privileged.
Never a brand standard for who I am.
But the truth.

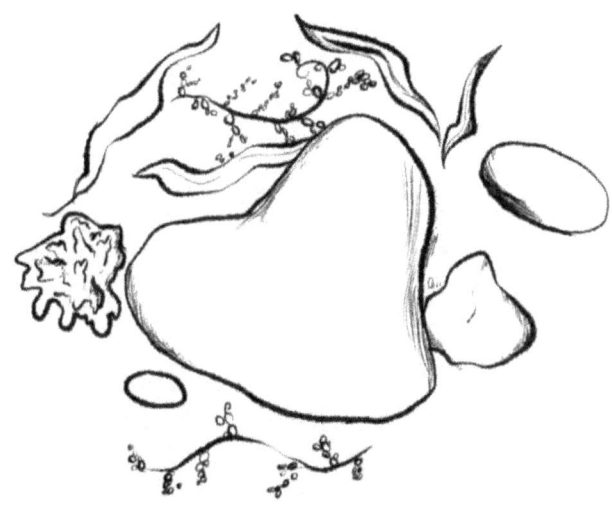

Abrasion - Larger Impacts

I deserve to heal at my own pace.

You'll Get There

If my knowledge falls short
battling with the latitude of waves
to get from the sea to land.

I'll take a seat
I'll listen
and reroute.

To weather the storm
and avoid cliffs entirely.

Samantha Elizabeth Parrell

I am empathetic
to a fault.

I absorb emotions like sea foam.

You'll Get There

I've learned over the years
that abrasive words
hit like waves.

So, I've prepared myself
for the larger fragments to hit.

Samantha Elizabeth Parrell

You'll find me
at the base of the cliff
with a heavy heart.

You'll Get There

Those months in the fog
wondering when it would clear.

Those days when it does
wondering how long it will last.

Samantha Elizabeth Parrell

A small greeting at the headland.

The thought that
no one should sit
so close to the shoreline
alone.

Little did I know
that what mattered to me
would be dissolved into foam
when I focused on your heavy heart.

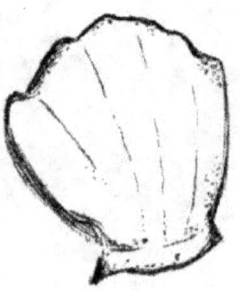

You'll Get There

Sometimes the sunrise isn't enough
you have to create
a beautiful sunset
in order for them to enjoy your company.

Samantha Elizabeth Parrell

What if I told you
that every soul you connected with
throughout your entire journey
would live in different parts of this world.

Would you yearn to travel
or be content knowing
they mean just as much to you there
as they do when they are home.

You'll Get There

The value of someone else's opinion
weighs heavy
like an undertow.

Fear, panic, exhaustion.

I can keep myself afloat
by being self aware.

Samantha Elizabeth Parrell

Guilt is a sign
it's your inner thoughts
being overshadowed.

You're trying to fit in
with the whispers of the wind
that travel from the mouths
of strangers to your soul.

You'll Get There

Being alone
comes naturally
when you dig deep
and accept yourself.

That is your first step.

Samantha Elizabeth Parrell

Take a walk in the woods.

Feel like you're slipping off the edge of the cliff?

It's okay to hit Nero.

All of those heavy thoughts
caused the abrasion.

You'll Get There

SPACE

Samantha Elizabeth Parrell

The battle between
morale's and a want.

Your base weight
carrying your morale's around
while you want to unpack
the importance of each want.

You'll Get There

Not everyone is replaceable.

Valuing your own self worth is important.

Being vulnerable is okay.

Feeling insecure isn't a fault.

You'll Get There

Putting yourself first
shouldn't feel like
you're creating a monster
in the mirror.

Samantha Elizabeth Parrell

Caring about the work you do
can conquer
the negative thoughts
that linger
like a storm cloud over a ship
steady on the ocean's edge.

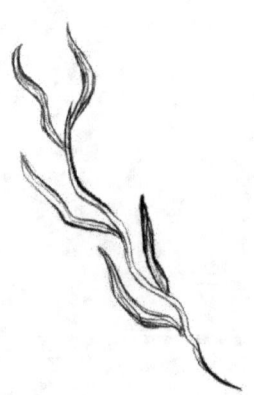

You'll Get There

You hurt their level of empathy.

Let them heal
in their own way.

Realize
that it may not include you
in their personal growth.

Samantha Elizabeth Parrell

A faint recollection
slowly disintegrating.

Social Anxiety
has risen
to remind me
that it really happened.

You'll Get There

I'd advocate
for you
and our basic rights.

With the hope that
it brings sleep
during those awful windy nights.

To live
with a little less fog
near the watershed.

To be able to admire
the sunset and sunrise.

In the shoe
on that cliff
we'll always be in your corner

Samantha Elizabeth Parrell

My priority is my inner calm.

Acknowledgements

To my readers, thank you for holding a space for my thoughts. The courage I gathered to place my words on paper for others to read was a daunting task.

For those of you who have encouraged me throughout this entire process, whether you knew you were a part of it or not, my gratitude is yours. You're fierce, honest and your relentless support is appreciated, truly.

The deepest form of friendship is the comfort of talking to an individual and instantly feeling a connection. Megan, thank you for bringing my words to life through your illustrations. Our matched energy made this a seamless experience. Your creativity is one that I am astonished by.

About the author

Samantha Elizabeth Parrell is a Canadian poet who grew up in a quaint town, in Newfoundland. She went to university to pursue her love for helping others, and ended up declaring her bachelor of arts in English and Geography. She has since found a passion for Fund Development and Communications, raising awareness and funds to help provide accessible and inclusive recreation programs, and career and educational services for people with disabilities. Samantha will continue to give back to the community, through her love of making and creating connections with people.

After sharing her love for writing over the years, this will be Samantha's first attempt at self-publishing her collection of poetry, *You'll Get There* at the age of thirty three.

Samantha's writing is a reflection of her experiences. Sit with her, as she becomes self aware and honest with who she is, leaving room for growth, always.

Resources

Bridge The Gapp
bridgethegapp.ca

Provincial CHANNAL Warm Line
1-855-753-2560 9:00am to 12:00am daily.

Mental Health Crisis Line
1-888-737-4668

Crisis Text Line (powered by Kids Help Phone)
Adults: Text 'WELLNESS' to 741741
Youth: Text 'HOME' to 686868
Text 'FRONTLINE' to 741741

Kids Help Phone
Call 1-800-668-6868
Visit <u>KidsHelpPhone.ca</u> for online resources

www.ingramcontent.com/pod-product-compliance
Lightning Source LLC
Chambersburg PA
CBHW072203100526
44589CB00015B/2347